SCREW CHOCOLATE 2

YYC QUEER WRITERS

CURATED BY M. JANE COLETTE

SCREW CHOCOLATE 2
14(+2) QUEER valentines to get you through February 14
by YYC Queer Writers
curated by M. Jane Colette
photography by Leslie Pringle

GENRES were made to be BROKEN
121, 104-1240 Kensington Rd NW
Calgary, Alberta T2N3P7 Canada

ISBN: 978-1-7751809-4-4 (trade paperback)
ISBN: 978-1-7751809-5-1 (e-book)
mjanecolette.com/ScrewChocolate

For Sam and Crystal

You see, it happened like this:

Sam: We have a Valentine's poem for you.

Crystal: We just wrote it.

Sam: Listen.

Crystal: "Roses are red..."

Sam: "Violets are blue..."

Crystal: "You're a big, stinky..."

Sam: "Poo."

Jane: ...

Sam: So can we be in the book?

Jane: No.

Crystal: Not even if we make if fancier, better?

Jane: No.

Sam: But we worked really hard on this.

Crystal: It was a good two minutes.

Jane: No.

Sam: But it's my birthday. And I won't write about love and Valentines and all that shit. But I want to be in the book.

Jane: I'll see what I can do.

I'm so fucking accommodating. xo *mjanecolette*

CONTENTS

BENIGN BEGINNINGS

M. JANE COLETTE

The girl is 10, 13 years younger than I am; blue hair, brown eyes, unfurrowed skin. She's also half a foot shorter. *Why do they all have to be so short?* my inner primal sub/outer femme moans. *How is this going to work? How much suspension of belief am I going to have to engage in to imagine...*

Editor: Unfurrowed? Is that a word?

Jane: Could you just read the piece through once without interrupting its flow with questions?

She smiles.

Her smile lights up a room. She knows this; she tells me so later.

It makes tears swim in my eyes, and I cry.

She crawls across the cushions of the Moroccan restaurant from her corner of the booth-tent to mine, and into my armpit and then over it, and suddenly I'm enveloped in her tiny arms.

Sumptuous cleavage.

Oh.

Holy fuck.

Those are... really fabulous breasts.

I am suddenly a 12-year-old boy or a genderless infant. I am perfectly soothed.

I rest my wet cheek on the bare exposure of flesh below the neck, above the plunge.

Pillows. Perfection.

> *Editor: Pillows?*
>
> *Jane: You know what would be nice? If you weren't so fucking judgemental about every single one of my word choices.*

She holds me. Asks questions I don't want to answer, but I do anyway, voice stained with tears. Fighting to keep them back. Losing. Then she says things. About my tears, sort of. About the cure for them. Which she promises — well, not promises, *suggests* — is hidden in those breasts.

Her somewhat twisted mind.

I caress the blue hair.

Hot tears.

Burrow into her neck and suddenly tears transform into lust and desire.

Kiss.

Lick.

Bite.

She moans as the waitress — who is nice but talks too much and needs a different kind of shampoo — brings our dessert.

"I want to touch you in all sorts of inappropriate ways," I murmur.

She spreads her scarf so I can.

We will never be able to come to this restaurant again, I think, as my fingers replace my wet cheek on her skin.

Her breath quickens.

She describes herself to me as an asexual — "Fine, a greysexual" — whose response to sex is... well, intellectual. Curious.

Not passionate.

She uses phrases such as borrowed arousal, mirrored desire.

"I know which algorithms to run to provide the expected response."

She also tells me she's a benign sociopath — first I think it's because she thinks that's what I want to hear — and then I think, indeed, that's what a sociopath would say under these circumstances — and I laugh through my tears.

She tells me about her other lovers. Romantic partners, she calls them.

And sexual partners. The handful of penises she's willing to put in her mouth. As opposed to the dozens and dozens that can penetrate her very tight pussy, even when half-flaccid.

Dozens and dozens and dozens of Tinder dates; she has perfected the science of the one night stand.

She has very beautiful lips, and I have searing pain in my chest-throat-belly-head.

It disappears when I drop my face to her neck.

Returns when I emerge.

Pain.

Tears.

She seems to like the tears.

> *Editor: Does she now?*
>
> *Jane: She does.*
>
> *Editor: Fuck. Jane. Not again.*
>
> *Jane: Just read.*

We first meet the day before I return to work on a work-in-progress novel. The novel exists as two drafts, both bad and inadequate, and one idea — brilliant.

She exists as a Bumble profile:

> *I am a professional who loves to have fun and meet new people. Also food. Kink/poly/pan. :)*
>
> *Also, a Unicorn.*

I swipe right with no expectations or excitement. Clinical

detachment. Perhaps I think, "Pretty child." Perhaps I think, "Mmm, too young."

Also, "Ugh, spiders!"

She is caressing a tarantula in one of her profile photographs.

But we match.

She writes:

> *We seem to have a lot in common! Nice to meet you :)*

I respond, half-lie, I suppose, but it sounds like truth:

> *Hello! I was hoping we'd match. Nice to meet you too.*

We meet a few days later, at 10 pm in a sheesha lounge. She's allergic to tobacco. We leave.

That day, she's full of frustration and angst.

I listen.

I am... interested. But unengaged. Cold.

Like a psychopath. Clinical.

> *Editor: I don't like where this is going.*
>
> *Jane: Hush. Just read.*

Pain. Searing.

Tears. Dammed.

They don't come until she drops me off at home and I crawl into bed beside you. I'm not sure you hear them. I hope you don't. After all, I dam them, hide them, for you.

Editor: Who is 'you'?

Jane: You don't need to know.

Editor: Extra character. Unnecessary. Kill it.

Jane: Fuck you. Today, I keep all my darlings.

There will be another meeting. I think? Maybe? I'm not sure. Perhaps I am another scalp, another notch on her metaphoric bedpost — I don't mind. I like being on a benign sociopath's bucket list. Perhaps she will be my methadone. Or at least anaesthesia.

She promises — no, she does not promise, *suggests* — that she could be medicine. Even a cure.

Pain. Tears.

Lick. Kiss.

Drown in scent, experience, distraction.

Delicious.

Her text:

Hey, what's your schedule like this week?

I think:

You can have me any night except for Tuesday and Friday. Choose.

It will end — all things end — badly or goodly.

Editor: ~~Goodly~~. Well.

Jane: Goodly.

I don't mind.

Tears.

I have two story titles, outlines, out of the experience already:

Stoking a horny asexual's desires

Flaccid penis whisperer

She wants to be my muse. More.

I want you to use me, she says. Her smile lights up the room; it's not the reason I cry.

I kiss the brown eyes. Caress the blue hair.

"You see... I have a thing for psychopaths," I confess.

"That's why," she says and envelops, drowns me in her flesh, pheromones, and the echo of feelings I know are only my own, "what you need now is a benign psychopath who does no harm."

I surrender.

Editor: This ends badly.

Jane: Or goodly.

Regardless. It ends.

Everything ends.

But first, it begins.

~

***M. Jane Colette** hates her editor, with a passion that is both narcissistic and borders on dysfunctional true love. Her published 'is it literature or is it porn' novels include* Tell Me, Consequences (of defensive adultery), Cherry Pie Cure, *and* Messy Christmas. *She's also the author of the non-fiction collection of essays on language, taboos, and the business of writing,* CUNT versus PUSSY *(reissued in 2017 with the more library-friendly title* Rough Draft Confessions*). Connect with @mjanecolette on Twitter and Instagram or whisper secrets to her at TellMe@mjanecolette.com.*

DEAR SARAH

DANA STAN

You pull me in close
and love falls from your lips
winding its way through my veins
until I feel you in my heart

our fingers braid themselves together
like the long hair of the little girls that we used to be
on the playground
that hair we reluctantly kept to feel normal
now normal seems so flat and grey
in the mountainous expanse of your open arms

you lend me a space in your heart
knowing that I am human and fallible
that I could corrode it from the inside
not knowing that I often shake
afraid to touch the smoothness of your skin
or to feel the warmth of your breath
because it whispers of a magnificence
I can't fully comprehend

~

***Dana Stan** is still working on her second novel and she's really got to finish it. Soon.*

PLAY

HP LONGSTOCKING

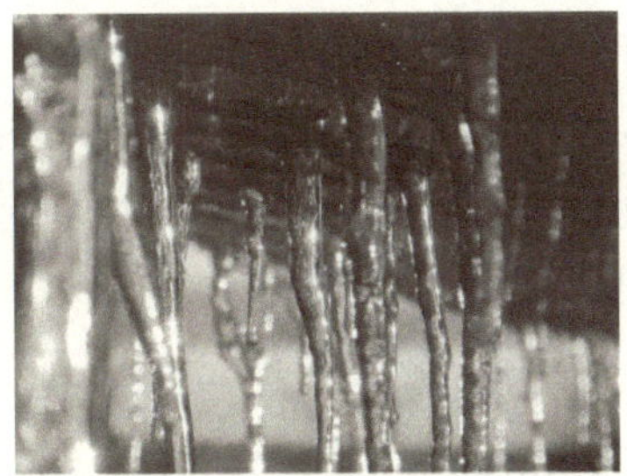

"What are we going to see!" I demand.

"You'll see." The infuriating answer.

"Tell me what kind of play this is! I need to prepare. Am I going to cry? Do I wear my sob sweater? Is it funny? Tell me!"

She only smiles.

Damn, my heart flutters every time I see that smile, but I push away my swoon response and remember — I am annoyed with her.

"I will dress you," she says.

This is not unexpected. Clothes are not my thing: buying them, washing them, choosing them, even wearing them. I'd rather not bother.

Her clothing choice is unexpected.

"What is wrong with my sports bra?" I grump as I pick up the black lacy contraption she bought me for my birthday, and which I've only worn twice.

"For me." She smiles, that sweet mischief directed at me.

I change.

"I'm uncomfortable," I tell her. "How am I going to enjoy this play if my clothes aren't comfy? You're going to pay for this."

I'm pouting, but trying to look cute. I'm rewarded by her eyes drifting up and down my body, now wrapped in scant layers of lace and leather.

"You'll enjoy it. It's exactly your kind of thing."

I get in the car, feeling strange in the passenger seat.

"One last thing to put on," she says and she slides the silk scarf off her neck and ties it over my eyes. It smells like her. I am caressed by warm silky peppermint and vanilla memories. Memories of silky skin, so edible, so warm. I am imagining what I will use the scarf for when the play is over. How I will tie her up, slowly-so-slowly, and punish or reward her for this evening — depending on how much I enjoy this play.

This surprise Valentine's play.

"We're here." She opens my door and grabs my hands to pull me up. I pull one free and pinch her nipple through her thin top.

I have excellent aim, even when blindfolded.

"That's what you get for blindfolding me," I say.

"Shh!"

She leads me up the stairs and helps me to my seat. We are just in time. The lights dim and I hear the crowd murmurs dying down to an anticipatory hush.

A spotlight clicks and I feel the heat of it as my blindfold is slipped off.

I am on stage.

So is she.

And so are all of our toys.

~

HP Longstocking *is slightly talented at many things. She enjoys studying science, painting, writing, dancing, and ranting, never letting mediocrity or public embarrassment stop her. Her inability to follow rules that don't make sense has taken her on adventures from fundamentalism to feminism, from Taiwanese prisons to marching in the streets.*

Chaotic good.

RRRR

T

I'm in a mood. Angsty and rowdy and downing whiskey like it's medication. Five bars later, I make out with the hottest kid at the club. Yes, kid. (Okay, 26. Still. Kid.) We are surrounded by high schoolers pretending to be adults and I've been gyrating on the speakers like it's my job, shirt tied up circa eighteen-year-old-me.

The ugly lights flicker honest over sticky floors and sticky limbs and my girlfriend and I leave to mill outside the bar. Hot Kid finds me again. I have hands on his massive biceps, palms on his broad chest, pushing emptily at his advances.

He wraps himself around me, sharing secrets and every bit of his practiced persuasion.

"I have a big dick," he says. "You won't be disappointed."

I am unconvinced.

...until some chubby kid pushes my Hot Kid between cabs on 2 am streets and a fight ensues. Shirts get discarded and so do my reservations. Damn, son. I'm a sucker for trash and muscles.

He does have a big dick. I am disappointed. The sex is perfunctory and he has a hard time listening to instructions. I want protection but he takes me and the risk anyway. When he tells me, "We can make this a thing," I laugh.

Hell, no, Hot Kid.

We leave his house on a rollercoaster red-light run. I have never driven through such a fun number of red lights before. Midway off the highway, his door and the hood is open and his beautiful, lean commando body are hustling to get some sort of spark going. We only "stop" to turn around and rescue my grandma's necklace at his place.

"Can I get it to you later?"

I raise an eyebrow. "When?"

I leave him with a kiss on the cheek and a thank you, feeling so much more Queen again. Close a rusty red door on some Hot Kid and a bad mood and walk away.

~

T is deep undercover, except when she bares all at boysboysboysandt.wordpress.com.

WILL IT SNOW?

ALYSSA LINN PALMER

"Do you think it'll snow again this year?" Vee asks me, her blue hair with its frosted white tips ("like snow," she said yesterday when she got it done) mashed to one side of her head from sleep, as she looks out the window and down to the streetlights and empty sidewalks below.

New York in the winter can be truly ugly when it hasn't snowed in a while.

Filthy ugly.

I keep hoping it will snow, even with the likely chaos that will follow.

But that's not really what I worry about. Bills, bills, bills. Freelancing can be tight at any time of year, but post-Christmas is often the worst, February especially, as clients tighten their belts. Thank God for my inherited apartment, for my nest egg, and for Vee. Without her, I'd be in a very dark, lonely place.

"I don't know," I say, realizing I haven't answered her.

"I hope so," Vee replies, coming to curl up on the sofa next to me, her head resting on my shoulder. Seeing us, one might think we were mother and daughter, though we're actually lovers. This May-December romance I expected to be brief has now lasted several years. "Aren't you coming to bed, Alex?"

"Soon," I promise, as I always do. "This article just needs finishing." My laptop is open on the coffee table, and the article there needs one more edit before I send it off.

"I'll come get you if you're not in bed in ten minutes," Vee says, rising. She bends to kiss me, and I savour the touch of her lips, the brush of the lip ring that she added this year, to go with her Monroe stud.

"I'll be there." The desire simmers in me after even that briefest of kisses, and I wonder if I'll ever lose that feeling, that near-constant desire for Vee.

I turn my focus back to the article, skimming through it, though the words are a blur. I send it off to the managing editor and I'm on my feet and in the bedroom well before the ten minutes are up.

But once I slide into bed with Vee, both of us deliciously

naked, my brain still won't quiet down. Money, bills, plans... Vee curls up next to me, warm and cosy and sleepy, and I'm sure I'll be awake all night.

~

Except I must sleep, because I wake to a bright room. Vee's side of the bed is empty. I sit up and stretch. Vee pops her head around the door.

"Alex! It did snow! Come on!" She comes into the room, and she's already dressed and looks ready to go out. Thick leggings, a mid-length heavy black skirt, fingerless gloves, and her down jacket. Her hair is all spiky, and this morning, the frosted tips look like snow.

"Give me a few minutes," I plead. "I just woke up."

"Ten minutes," Vee says, "that's all. But I'll buy you breakfast. Come on, let's get out there before someone else ruins it all."

I dress, picking out my warmest clothes, and go through to the bathroom for a quick ablution. I think it takes me fifteen minutes. Vee is pacing by the front door when I exit. She's pulled on her boots and when she sees me, she grins. She has my coat ready, and my boots are sitting out, along with my pashmina scarf and a decent pair of gloves. Once I'm dressed and we're out the door, Vee takes my hand. She's so excited she's practically skipping down the hallway. When we get to the ground floor, she steps outside and out from under the canopy, and turns her face to the sky. A few flakes are still floating, and she catches one on her tongue.

"Let's go to the park," I say, giving her hand a tug. We set off for Central Park, some blocks from us, but it's a quiet walk today. The snow has scared everyone inside except for a few other hardy souls. The sidewalks are cleared, mostly. The squeaky crunch of snow under our boots is a welcome sound.

We enter the park near the Strawberry Fields memorial for John Lennon. It hasn't been cleared off yet, and I can see the bumps in the snow from candles and flowers, left over from the December 8th memorial. The benches are empty, silent, themselves covered. I've rarely seen Central Park so quiet. The trees are heavy with snow too, muffling the sound of traffic.

"This is beautiful," Vee murmurs, her hand still tight in mine. We walk slowly, heading towards Sheep Meadow, Vee's favourite place. Open and wide, or as wide as you'll get in New York City. Vee says she can pretend she's on a farm, or in the country, there. Me, I just like watching Vee's delight. And experiencing mine. It's almost Valentine's Day, and I'm here with Vee. She lets go of my hand and runs out into the meadow, her boots slipping on the snow. I walk after her more carefully, then I bend to pick up a handful of snow, an idea sliding into my mind.

A naughty idea.

The snow packs easily since it's not very cold. Perfect snow-ball temperature. I haven't thrown a snowball in years, but with luck, my aim will be true. I wait, watching until Vee has come within range, yet is not looking at me.

I let fly, and it grazes her shoulder. She turns, laughing, bending to scoop up her own ball. Before she can finish, I've scooped and made a second and sent it off, and she has to duck. She's giggling like a madwoman, and my grin is so wide my cheeks ache. I keep going, making a third snowball. Vee lets hers fly, but her giggles have put her aim off, and it goes wide. I throw the third, and it hits her midriff. She throws another, and this time, she gets me, straight in the chest. The snow splatters, and I shake my head.

Vee bounds closer. "Sorry, Alex!" she calls out as she run-slides towards me. When she gets an arm's length away, she does slip, and we crash down into the snow together. I can feel the snow melting through my jeans, and I know I'll be cold soon, but it doesn't matter. Vee and I are here, she's with me, I'm with her. I cup her cheek, reddened from the cold, and kiss her.

The kiss is more than brief, one more suited to privacy, not the middle of a snowy field, but I don't care. We kiss until my head swims, and the shock of Vee's cold hand on my breast inside my jacket startles me. Her thumb rubs over my nipple, hardening it immediately. I want more, but here? I've never been an exhibitionist, yet now, with Vee...

Vee pulls back, unzipping my coat further, until it's splayed open. I shiver with the chill, but she covers me with her body, her hand sliding down my front, swiftly unbuttoning my jeans, unzipping them. Her fingers are still cool when she slips them into my underwear, but not for long. I arch against her touch, wanting more as she slides a finger inside me.

"My favourite things," Vee murmurs in my ear. "You and the snow. You're beautiful like this, Alex. So beautiful. And mine."

It doesn't take long before I'm there, trembling on the edge. Two years and she still affects me like this. Even with the wet soaking into my jeans, I'm wetter between my legs than anywhere else. Vee dips her head and kisses me, then moves to my neck, what little of it is bare beneath the pashmina.

Distantly I hear voices, then only the wind, and Vee's breath. She flicks her thumb over my clit, steady and knowing, and that's it.

I'm pretty sure I see stars.

Though maybe it's snow. Or Vee's hair.

She's all I need.

"Tomorrow is Valentine's Day," Vee murmurs into my ear. "This is just the beginning."

I forget my cold legs, the melting snow seeping into my jeans, forget everything but her and me and us and love.

***Alyssa Linn Palmer** writes romantic noir, lesbian romance, and a variety of short stories. Her novel* Betting on Love *was a finalist for a Rainbow Award in 2015, and in 2016, her novel* Midnight at the Orpheus *won a Rainbow Award for Best Bisexual Fiction. Find her works at alyssalinnpalmer.com, and all the usual online retailers. Want to chat? She's on Instagram and Twitter as @alyslinn, and on Facebook as herself.*

If you want more of Alex and Vee, check out Vee: Volume 1, *and the free stories available on her website.*

SHITTY FEMINIST, NOT

DALLAS BARNES

Valentine's Day was not made for feminists like me. It's a stupid holiday created for the sole purpose of selling overpriced, bejewelled cards, steroid-injected roses, and highly flammable lingerie sewn by overseas children who are barely old enough to walk. It's also this overwhelming override of all things liberation, as millions of First World women wait with bated breath for their men to declare their love with dinners at overpriced restaurants and a night of missionary positions and the eleven o'clock news. I pride myself on being the feminist that hates Valentine's Day. I pride myself on my independence from the commercialism of love.

Some days, I am a shitty feminist.

I lied when I said that I pride myself on my independence from the commercialism of love. Well, more like... I stretched the truth. Through the kick-assery of my feminist vows, at times I slip for the sake of self-care. Some people in times of strife go straight for the chocolate, while some make it a point to conquer every single vagina in a ten-mile radius. I, on the other hand, keep both my mouth and legs closed and curl up on my cherry-red IKEA couch, press play, and indulge in the admittedly white-washed, privileged world of four fictional women who drink way too many sugary drinks, and waste their self-proclaimed female empowerment on the prospect of the male gaze.

Carrie, Miranda, Samantha, and Charlotte of *Sex and the City* are my chocolate and vaginas.

Carrie, Miranda, Samantha, and Charlotte are the epitome of the commercialism of love.

Why do I have such a fascination with *Sex and the City*? My love of all things New York is definitely a contending reason. The Manolo Blahniks dazzle my eyes, completely privileged, materialistic, and over-priced indulgence that they are. Carrie couldn't afford a down payment on her apartment, yet had $20,000 worth of shoes in her closet? Yes, she did.

The men who dominate each episode dampen my adoration. However, Samantha hooked up with a chick once, and Mr. Big's reluctance to commit always resonated with me.

I don't know why I have seen each episode at least five times, and both movies at least a dozen. Why I continue to wear my pink pussy hat in the day and watch the girls wear vintage Halston sari-inspired dresses and vintage turbans while visiting Abu Dhabi (with local man servants catering to their every need) is beyond my liberal thought process.

Feminism is a funny thing. It can follow a strict code of conduct that is often above and beyond what the typical human adheres to. Makeup, for example, can be a tricky thing. Cat-eyes and mascara that adds volume and separates each lash can be problematic. Subscribing to enhancements in order to make oneself more 'pretty' has feminist backlash written all over it. We are all beautiful creatures as we are and the enhancement of oneself can be a reinforcement of the manufactured ideal of beauty. People spend countless amounts of money and have disfigured themselves in the pursuit of this manufactured perfection. In *Sex and the City,* Samantha has that issue numerous times with laser treatments to her face that result in rashes that ruin her party plans for the night…

So. Makeup bad. Right? But... what about a woman's right to express herself with no limits? Doesn't that include makeup? Cosmetic surgery? A boob job? When Samantha decides on a boob job, her plans are thwarted by a diagnosis of breast cancer after the surgeon discovers a lump. Just saying.

Although the show is built around the four main female characters, in actuality its premise is all things Carrie and her experiences while writing her column 'Sex and the City.' I find myself comparing my life to hers all the time. Like that time(s) when Mr. Big could not commit, or when Aidan bought her a pear-shaped diamond, and even the time when she registered herself at Manolo Blahnik in an attempt to prove that stolen $400 shoes were indeed important regardless of the fact that her friend told her to worry about more serious things like children.

Of course I was not wearing $400 shoes, nor was I ever

offered a pear-shaped diamond, but I was touched by the sentiment that not all women need to have children to feel complete, or that a partner's choice in jewelry should indeed be a reflection of knowing you as a person.

But I don't think it's Carrie alone who draws me to *Sex and the City*. It's how she exists in relation to her girlfriends: it's the complex relationship amongst Carrie, Miranda, Samantha, and Charlotte that compels me to watch day after day.

What is most remarkable about the quadruple friendship is that they respect each other for who they are. There is a love between them like no other. In fact, when he finally realized that Carrie was 'the one,' Big begged and pleaded with the girls to tell him truthfully if he should get her in Paris where she was shacking up with the annoyingly dull and egotistical Russian. While they were drilling him about his true intentions and past indiscretions, he surprised them all by saying, "You three know her better than anyone. You're the loves of her life. Any guy would be lucky enough to come in fourth."

Like seriously, how fucking beautiful is that? I swear, that is my favourite line ever, from everything — period. I think about it almost daily. How fucking remarkable.

So while I turn my nose up at Valentine's Day, I also give you the story of a love between a girl and her tv show… which is also a story about a girl and her feminism, or the most beloved story of a girl and her besties.

What I do know is that I love this show for reasons I question every day. But that is my own prerogative. And if anything, I love that weirdness about me.

~

***Dallas Barnes** is a queer, cisgender, feminist, activist, and writer. She writes about life — its downfalls, turmoils, hilarities, and elations. Her experience with mental illness and all things queer makes her writing real, raw, and in your face. Dallas lives in Calgary, Alberta, with her cat Grizzly and tweets as @salladsenrab.*

ODE TO ME

TANYSIA KOMERS

Ode to me: the ski bunny.
The woman with the legs.
With the smile, frost sitting deep in dimples.
Helmet flying orange through bowed branches
Green on black on so much happy white powder.
Pink lips, soft skin.
Calves like springboards,
Breath booming, heart pounding.

Sweat cold, ice sharp.

Ode to me: the ski bunny.

The woman with the arms.

With the waist, hot dropping new lines and soft bumps.

Air growing beneath wood and above cliffside.

Fear in failure in success in launching happy white powder.

Long limbs, strong levers.

Thighs like thunder,

Hot neck, fresh cheeks.

Sweat cold, ice sharp.

Ode to me; the ski bunny.

The woman with the vision.

With the smile, frost sitting deep in dimples.

***Tanysia Komers** is a tall thing with itchy fingers and a tendency to say more than she should. She thinks she's a writer some days, but most days she's lost somewhere in her pursuit of peaks: business, mountains, adrenaline... She is a wannabe athlete with the kind of heartbreak that only comes from being benched for the season and is taking it out on her keyboard. Maybe next year, you'll find this ski bunny on the slopes again.*

14 FACTS AND/OR FICTIONS REGARDING THE MIDDLE

L. SARA BYSTERVELD

One

As a child, "the middle" was my favourite spot. I had one sister, who passed away when she was nineteen and I was eight, so even before she died, with only two of us kids in the family, there was no middle normally. It was only when travelling with friends or cousins that I could call dibs on the prime (only to me) middle spot in the backseat or on the couch.

I liked to be sandwiched between two people who loved me.

It was cozy.

two

Frankie Muniz is not able to remember any of his time playing the character of Malcom on *Malcolm in the Middle.* He assumes this lapse in memory is due to the nine concussions and "fair amount of mini strokes" he has suffered.

three

At my grandmother's funeral, my two partners sat on either side of me and I held hands with both of them. We were in my hometown, which is very small (not big enough to be a town, actually), and I didn't know who knew about our relationship.

I didn't care.

My grandma had died; I was entitled to the comfort I needed. I let my terrible uncle look down on us holding hands while he ranted about himself in the guise of some sort of eulogy. I hope he saw us, but I'm not sure. I was staring at the choir and repeating to myself, "I am a leaf on the wind."

four

I grew up in rural central Alberta, where wedding dances consisted mainly of country music and also Bob Seger, who may or may not qualify as country music. There was a reliable staple of songs that played at every wedding over the years, including "Daddy's Hands," "The River," "Fishin' in the Dark" and a catchy little number that went,

> "I'd start walkin' your way, you'd start walkin' mine. We'd meet in the middle 'neath that old Georgia pine. We'd gain a

> lot of ground, 'cause we'd both give a little. And there ain't no road too long, when you mee-eet in the middle."

five

Being caught in the middle when your two loves are bickering or even fighting is a position that is at once relatively safe and very uncomfortable. You can be thankful that you're not personally the target of anyone's ire, but at the same time, you're busy listening to, validating, and supporting each of them while trying not to make things any worse. Options for coping in this situation include becoming an expert mediator, playing both sides to your advantage (not recommended) or disappearing until they sort it out.

six

"The middle of nowhere" is either somewhere you're trying to escape, or somewhere you're trying to get back to. When you grow up in the middle of nowhere, you spend your life dreaming of getting away to somewhere like Paris or New York, where something is always happening and you're always surrounded by people. Once you've been surrounded by people for a few years, you either start saving up for a place in the middle of nowhere or you pay good money to vacation in the middle of nowhere once a year.

seven

From what I can surmise, it's common to have an extramarital affair during mid-life, a period which the Internet seems to define as 40-65. This gives me hope, because as some of us reach our late 30s, we start to wonder whether anyone will ever find our stress-ravaged, cheese-bloated, parenting-aged body attractive again. If so many people are having affairs after 40, people over 40 must find each other attractive.

On a related note, I have to wonder when more middle-aged people will just give polyamory a try. When we millennials reach middle age, I suppose.

eight

The correct way to eat an Oreo cookie is to gently twist apart the two wafers and then lick off all the icing from the middle. Dipping the wafers in milk before eating is a nice touch but not totally necessary if, for instance, you are on a picnic.

nine

The phrase "in the middle of something" does not refer to a physical location nor to being literally in the middle of anything. Rather, it's something we say when we are working on a task that is complex or complicated — or a euphemism for things we aren't able to or don't want to explain.

For instance, imagine that drama has erupted among several of your employees and you call a meeting to address the situation.

The phone rings; it's your spouse.

"I'm in the middle of something, dear, I'll have to call you back," you say.

"I'm in the middle of something" is a good brush-off for when you don't want to talk about the situation and you need to make it clear that you're tied up.

ten

The male partner in our triad will never stand in the middle when we pose for photos, because we all agree that it gives the appearance of a harem, which couldn't be further from the truth.

eleven

There are many creative and amusing ways to flip someone the bird. I recommend you learn a few and use them often. A personal favourite between my partners and me is one that mimes pulling a tube of lipstick out of your pocket, taking off the cap, applying the lipstick to your lips, recapping it, and putting it back in your pocket. The lipstick, of course, is your middle finger.

If you're a decent synchronized swimmer, an option with optimal impact is to flip both middle fingers while treading water with your feet, then slowly sinking beneath the surface while still holding them high. Go as low as you need to for the tips of your fingers to submerge, then slowly push back up until your head is fully out of the water again. Never lower the middle fingers, and maintain eye contact when not underwater. They'll be talking about it for years.

twelve

In roller derby, "up the middle" is a commonly heard directive. It refers to the fact that for the jammer (that's the skater from each team who has to break through the pack of blockers and circle the track, passing members of the opposing team to get points), the safest place to get through the pack is the centre of the track. If the jammer tries to pass the pack on the inner or outer edge of the track, the other team has a higher chance of knocking them out of bounds, and forcing them to skate back a legal distance before stepping back onto the track and trying again. The middle also happens to be a difficult place to break through, as the blockers are often more crowded together there and form a wall that can be formidable.

It's all about weighing the risks.

thirteen

When sleeping three to a bed, the middle is both a coveted and reviled spot. As my fiancée says, it's safe, like the middle of the track in roller derby — you don't risk losing your covers or falling off the bed (we recommend a king-sized bed or larger for triads) — but it's also difficult, because you can't move much and you get suffocatingly warm.

My fiancée always takes the middle because she is tough but also cuddly.

fourteen

When you first find yourself in a triad, the song "Stuck in the Middle With You" seems very apt and funny, until you realize that whoever the band was singing to is stuck between jokers and clowns *with* them, and you are now stuck between a joker and a clown, all by yourself, possibly forever.

~

__L. Sara Bysterveld__ answers to Lindsay (her very good reason for the pretentious pen name can be found on her author site, LSaraBysterveld.com), aside from when she doesn't answer at all *because she is hiding from her five kids/step-kids, two partners, and two cats. She was voted 'Most Likely to Publish a Book' and 'Most Likely to Be a Syndicated Columnist' by her peers at her college journalism graduation party, immediately before jumping into the pool fully clothed. She's currently working on the former with her non-fiction book,* Triads: How It Works When Love Includes Three.

Find out more about Lindsay, triads and the book on Instagram (@thetriadbook) or the website TheTriadBook.com.

14 MONTHS

ANN ZEE

Fuck you, fuck you, fuck you.

I know, how ridiculously lame.

I waited fourteen months for you...

The *it's not you, it's me* speech.

After 40 minutes you say, *Let go.*

Move on. You've already gone.

I waited fourteen months for you.

Jesus Christ,

I am a buffoon.

Greying roots.

Fading sight.

Bruised ego.

Aching heart.

Fuck...

Of course I chased.

After you, your complicated

azure eyes. Simplified

world views. Wanted to

move heaven to get

to you. Suffocated instead

for fourteen months

in hell. For you?

Fuck you, fuck you, fuck you.

And we didn't even.

I was just your vacation.

You were my destination.

I waited fourteen months for you.

Would have waited longer. For you.

I know, how ridiculously lame.

Fuck. You.

And... we didn't.

~

***Ann Zee** is an acupuncturist and practitioner of Chinese medicine. She grew up in Vancouver but has made Calgary her home for the past 25 years. She has enthusiastically volunteered with Camp fYrefly here in Calgary.*

Ann has participated in the Coming Out Monologues *and has facilitated a couple of events with Calgary's Lesbian and Queer Women's Meet Up group. She is also a member of the Calgary Sexuality & Gender Diversity CPS board where she is working to build bridges between all communities.*

This is Ann's first foray into presenting written work and she is excited to be in the company of some amazing writers who are boldly sharing their stories.

HEART-SHAPED DOUGH

CALLAN FIELD

"So, to summarize: two medium heart-shaped pizzas, one vegetarian with extra cheese, the other half-Tuscan and half-perogy, a bottle of our shittiest red wine, and no fucks about Western society's obnoxious notions of heteronormative serially monogamous elevator relationships on a holiday appropriated and popularized by capitalists who, through mass marketing, have conditioned us to believe that red roses combined with cute carcinogenic cards, inexplicable combinations of flavoured chocolates, gaudy gold jewelry and egregiously expensive dinners on one specific day of the year are the ultimate expression of true love while ignoring that today is the number one day to off yourself and that getting drunk at Boston Pizza while ordering Valentine's Day pizzas ironically with your best friend is simultaneously awesome and depressing?

"Oh, my bad, I totally forgot the part about how you heard on Radiolab that one million roses are grown annually just for today, emitting 9,000 metric tons of carbon dioxide and contributing to climate change which has resulted in it being ten degrees outside meaning there is no snow for you to go skiing on. Anything else?"

Our waiter finished his monologue like a radio professional, lightning fast, with crisp and clear intonation, each word dripping with sarcasm and emotional ennui, as though listening to his customers' conversations while waiting for them to make up their fucking minds about what to order and mocking them afterwards was a regular hobby of his. He put his small tomato sauce stained notebook and cyan Bic pen back into his server's apron. As he did, I was captivated by his perfectly painted pearl fingernails. He pretended to read our order from his notebook and I smiled a bit as I imagined the kitchen's reaction to such a ridiculous request.

A roar of laughter split our faces — I'd have typed it out as "bwahahaha" — and then, Zandra and I broke into a slow heavy applause. The sharp thuds echoing through the restaurant captured the attention of the assortment of couples who had chosen this romantic dining experience in Crowfoot Crossing, a strip mall in Calgary's northwest.

Among the awkward adolescent dates, I was pleased to spot a few queers. My favourite by far were the gay clones sitting at a tiny table kitty corner from us. They were wearing what I estimated to be five thousand dollar matching royal blue tuxedos and sporting identical low pompadour haircuts.

As I watched, the clones shared a bowl of pasta drowning in Parmesan cheese and repeatedly recreated the *Lady and the Tramp* kiss until they finally abandoned all pretense and just made out.

I had so many questions.

Our waiter's lips remained pursed, the deep purple plum lipstick forming a line that seemed to only indicate displeasure.

Zandra dove in, "Let me guess: double major in theatre and history? At… I'm going to say… McGill? And then after a few years of trying to make it as an actor, you couldn't pay your bills, so you moved into your parents' basement and do impromptu performances to stay fresh? As prep for open mic night? Not that I'm judging. We studied photography and look where that got us."

Zandra had a knack for figuring out people's life stories, and no qualms about being brutally direct with strangers. I recently realized she talked as a way of coping with her anxiety. She let her thoughts flow like a river without a dam.

#nofilter

Our waiter lifted one perfectly manicured eyebrow, and tilted his head a little to the left. Finally, he cracked and started to chuckle.

"Ya got me. Nice call on the basement."

"I love that I got that right. We'll add an order of calamari. That should pair nicely with our wine, existential dread, and critique of this disaster of a holiday."

"Good one!" I said. Zandra and I high-fived.

With the tiniest of curtsies, our waiter left.

"I thought he was gonna be so pissed with you."

"Naaaaaah, people like it when I'm a jerk to them."

I snorted. "Last time you did it, you got us thrown out of Sushi Boat... Sushi Boat!"

"But she started it!"

"True. Besides, I think it's hilarious. P.S. you missed the minor in Gender Studies." I passed her my phone. I found our waiter's official website; a modified Tumblr page.

Zandra took a look and snorted.

"Oh Gods, he was fucked the moment his parents named him Maximilian Valentina Jenius."

"Noooo, that can't be his real name."

"Sure is, he posted a photo of his passport on Facebook." Having done her sleuthing, Zandra returned my phone. Our wine arrived a moment later via a dull busser. I took a sip.

It was definitely their worst wine.

"Speaking of being fucked, I have a story for you."

"This better be good."

"Oh, trust me it is. So, this afternoon I had a play date with ROG" — Ripped Old Guy was the acronym I coined with my boyfriend for Dorian, a dominant Quebecois bodybuilder in his 50s with whom I'd been playing for the last few months — "and before that I had a dermatologist appointment. Like every time we play, ROG ordered me to arrive with my ass plugged."

"Butt plug, you mean?"

"Right. I have a really awesome metal one that is super-comfortable. It's actually called the World's Most Comfortable Butt Plug." We both chuckled.

"But I don't have time to go home after the appointment so I go to it plugged, which is fine. I've worn it out before. I can feel it inside me with every step and get an extra jolt when I sit down — it's pretty hot. I run a couple errands, and then park near the office downtown and as I'm getting out of the car, I feel a bit of wetness in my bum. Look at the car seat and it's dry. So, in my head, I go 'that's weird' and keep going. Then I'm riding a packed elevator up to the doctor's office, and all of a sudden, I realize it's probably because there's lube leaking out of my ass and I'm wearing a jock strap, so no underwear to soak it up. I'm the first one out of the elevator on the fifth floor, and all I can think of is that everyone behind me is staring at my ass. I immediately go to the bathroom and sure enough, there's this diamond shaped lube stain on my khaki pants."

Zandra chortled and refilled her wine glass.

"I try and dry it off with toilet paper, but that literally does nothing. The entire time I'm at the doctor's, I keep trying to position myself so that no one is behind me. At one point I get out of the exam chair and walk backwards instead of turning around. Thankfully it wasn't too cold today, so on the walk back to my car I wrapped my jacket around my waist to hide it."

"And how was ROG afterwards?"

"Holy fuck, so good. It's funny, he always wears leather head-to-toe in our sessions, except for these cute black fuzzy slippers and white socks. Anyway, as soon as I walked in the door, he ordered me to strip down to my jockstrap, put the collar around my neck and hooded me. The hood leaves my mouth open, and I worshipped his cock on all fours in his living room until he bound me to the sling in the basement. I spent the next two hours gagged, fed poppers and being fucked, it was greeeaat."

"Daaaaaamn, yeah that's hot. Look at you, Talfryn — a full-fledged homo! I feel like a proud mom. You going to see your sub sometime soon?"

Our pizzas arrived and I shrugged. "Hopefully. Scheduling fucking sucks."

"Ain't that the truth," Zandra said, and then dug into her heart-shaped pastry.

Three bottles later, Zandra left to pick up her girlfriend from work and I opened Grindr out of curiosity and boredom as I finished my wine. Online and ten feet away were the clones. A mischievous smile split my lips and instead of sending them a message, I wandered over to say hello. Partway through introductions my waiter returned, dropping a heavy pint onto the table with a thud. A single drop of ale flung onto the left clone's pant leg, where only the waiter and I could see it.

With a wink he walked away.

~

***Callan Field** is a queer Canadian artist, adventure(r) and dog lover – allergies be damned. An emerging visual artist, he studied environmental science before completing his BFA at Ryerson University in 2014. While his primary medium is photography, his work has expanded to include writing, video, and installation. He was recently selected for The Peel, a multi-layered project featuring six Canadian artists as they canoed into the Arctic Circle through* *the Peel River Watershed. The documentary and touring exhibition follows the journey of each artist as they express the experience through their unique medium. Learn more at thepeel.ca, and find out more about Callan at callanfield.com and @callanfield on Twitter and Instagram.*

REFLECTIONS THROUGH AN UNFROSTED FEBRUARY WINDOW

BROOKE NICHOLAS

I sit on the windowsill of my apartment, cuddled up in the blanket my grandma made for me.

I'm watching lovebirds come and go from the restaurant down the street. It's Valentine's Day and, watching their happy faces, full of love for one another, I reflect on all that has happened this past year and wonder what more there is to come.

The past year brought a great love that was unexpected but very needed for both lovers, and great loss as the love was not to last. The discovering of one's true self. That realization that even if we are born into the wrong body, with the right support and the letting go of fear, life is happier when we embrace who we are meant to be.

It brought the knowledge that sexuality is not a choice. And that even if we try to give up who we love most… that is not what happiness is about.

The hours tick by as I watch the street below.

I realize that even though I am not down on the street with them, sharing in the warming touch of a lover, I am happy.

Happier than I have been in a long time.

~

***Brooke Nicholas** grew up in a small BC town with her grandma. Came out when she was 15 when she met her first great love. Moved to the big city of Calgary when she was 20. Had a few other amazing women touch her life since then. But none that wanted to stay.*

DAMN I WISH I WAS YOUR LOVER

LOTIS CERVANTES

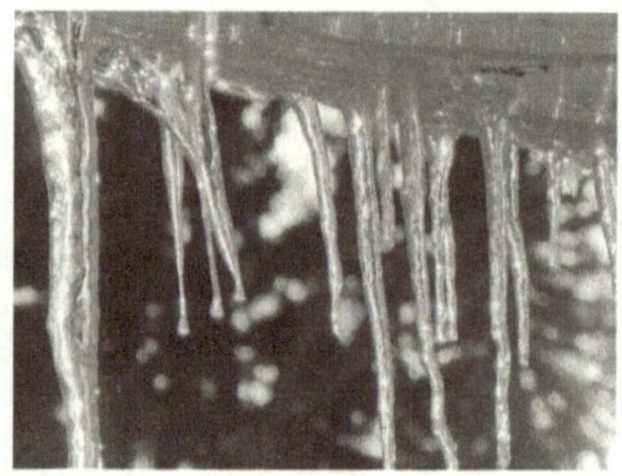

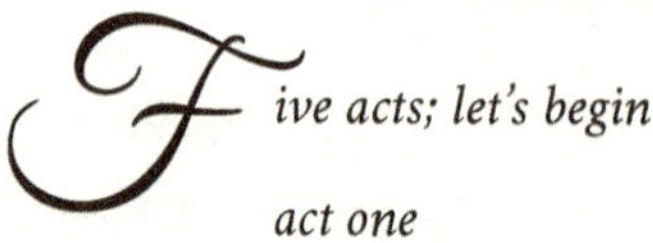

Five acts; let's begin

act one

Red hair reaching the top of your shoulders, soft pink lips that gently curl into a dimpled smile, light brown eyes that are warm as sunshine, and a small oval scar close to your temples that makes me wonder how it came about.

Were you precocious as a child?

Did you get scratched in the face, the incident leaving you a mark for life?

Was it chicken pox?

Did you pick on your skin even though you were warned not to?

I think of you a lot.

Since the first time I saw you walk into the coffee shop, you have been on my mind.

I remember cleaning the pastry glass display case when I saw your high heels. They were red.

When I looked up, there you were, standing in front of the counter. Smiling at me.

I just stood there, speechless, holding on to a dirty damp rag, unsure of what to do.

My coworker called out to you but you told her, it's fine.

That you will wait till I'm ready to serve you.

I rushed to the sink to wash my hands.

It's a cardinal rule at the coffee shop to wash and sanitize. I like following the rules. It makes me feel safe.

Plus, I don't want anyone to remind me of such a simple thing.

You ordered a medium coffee. Two sugars and no cream.

I don't know why my hands were shaking while I poured the hot liquid. I serve coffee to customers a hundred times a day. I can even do it with eyes closed.

Not that I would.

I gave you your order and our fingers touched briefly.

Did I imagine the tiny sparks I felt or was it static electricity?

If you asked me how I do my laundry, I swear I use dryer sheets.

You smiled, showing those dimples that just about killed me.

I'm a sucker for those.

They say it's an abnormality but who the fuck cares?

You paid with your credit card, tapping the machine when I said it was ready.

"Have a good day," you told me.

"You as well." My standard reply.

act two

Every day since then has been a good day.

You come to the coffee shop all the time, joining my line no matter how long it gets.

I'm not as nervous when I see you but I noticed a change in me.

I look forward to seeing you—at 10 in the morning, 12 pm, and then at 3.

You are a creature of habit, just like me.

I memorized your order. Now, you don't even have to say anything.

Except for that Monday morning. You ordered an everything bagel with plain cream cheese instead of your bacon breakfast sandwich.

It was a conversation starter.

You said you wanted to mix things up a bit.

I looked at your hair.

That's when I noticed it wasn't straight.

You had it curled and you still looked mighty fine.

I mentally gave you a thumbs-up sign.

You looked at the name on my badge.

"Jessica," you said with a smile. "I'm Kat."

act three

Now… I anticipate your visits.

My friends at work notice how extra cheerful I get.

I'm smiling all the time and there's a spring in my step.

They have no idea what goes on in my mind.

I wonder how it would feel to run my hand through your hair?

Is it silky, smooth, fragrant? Soft?

I imagine trailing my fingers on your creamy skin. That's soft, I know without touching.

Will my touch make you quiver?

The thought makes my heart beat fast and my palms sweaty.

How does it feel to kiss you?

If our lips touch, will my knees weaken under the weight of my attraction?

I really want to kiss you.

When you're standing in front of me, I stare at those full lips.

My breath hitches a little and I try not to make it seem so obvious.

Once you leave, I let go of the breath I'm holding.

act four

You've made me so distracted that people at work are starting to notice.

"Is it red?" a coworker asked when he found me staring at the boxes of coffee cups, forgetting what size I needed to restock the counter shelves.

"What?" I blinked, not hearing what he said.

"Red hair, pretty, dimples?" he grinned, a teasing look in his eyes.

I kept my mouth shut because I didn't know what to say.

"You won't be the first." He pulled a sleeve of small brown coffee lids and stood on his tiptoes to reach for a box of stir sticks.

"What do you mean, I won't be first?"

He placed the merchandise on top of the metal shelves.

"We've been in your shoes before," he answered.

"Why do I feel like you're going to tell me something I won't like?"

He smirked.

"Let's just say the fantasy is the best part."

What did he mean?

I didn't want to find out.

act five

On a snowy Wednesday morning, the line at the counter was longer than usual.

People were dressed in thick coats, standing close to each other. Bitching about the cold.

I was charged with making coffee and I didn't see you come in.

I saw you only when the cashier tapped me on the shoulder and pointed towards the door.

You were standing beside a brunette. Looking up, because she was taller than you.

Both of you were smiling and there was something different.

You looked happier. Like 'twinkle in your eyes' happy.

I tried to concentrate on the orders, hoping you wouldn't join my line this time.

The disappointment of seeing you with someone else hurt my mind. My heart.

But. You were a creature of habit.

"Where's Jessica?" you asked while I pretended to read an order on the screen. My back to you.

"She's here." My coworker pointed towards me.

You waved. I smiled while checking out the woman you were with.

She was looking at me too.

"What do you want, babe?" Your voice. To her.

I dropped the cup to the floor when I heard it.

I bent down in haste not only because I felt exposed but also because I felt the sting of disappointment in my cheeks.

They were red. Not from the heat of the coffee brewer but from shame.

I got up and made your order.

Medium coffee, two sugar, no cream.

Large chai tea with three milks, no sugar. For her.

Your usual order of bacon breakfast sandwich. This time, for two.

I wanted to escape, but I had to give you the drinks.

With a fake smile on my face, I handed you the steaming beverages.

"Thank you," you said before you walked to the corner to wait for your sandwiches.

The fantasy is the best part.

Now I know why.

~

Lotis Clemente Cervantes *lives in Calgary with her wife. She is a yoga enthusiast (?) and a creator of LGBT-themed stories written in Taglish (Tagalog/English) that veer toward sadness/drama... which she claims is not intentional. You can find her works at Wattpad.com/lccervantes.*

SHE WITH THEM

TET MILLARE

You are She
I am They
You with Me?
She with Them?

Our picture of We
Could be just like Theirs
If We wanted it to be—

Warm, tight hugs

Tender, sweet kisses

Late night walks along the river

For as long as

You hold Me as Me

And I hold You as You

The world will find that

She can be with Them too.

~

WRITER'S NOTE: Tet personally uses both the female pronouns *She/Her/Hers* and the gender-neutral pronouns *They/Them/Theirs.*

~

***Tet Millare** is a proud queer Filipino-Canadian LGBTQIA+ advocate, community volunteer, and adventurer. One of the founders of VOICES, Calgary's Coalition of Two-Spirit and Racialized LGBTQIA+ and a board member of Fairy Tales Queer Film Fest, she strives to live life in the present and channels her hopeless sentimental side through any expression of art. Tet has written and performed (sung, even!) at the* Coming Out Monologues, *danced with the M:ST8 (Mountain Standard Time Performative Art), and performed as a technical non-dancer at Fluidfest. She also works as a professional photographer — check out her work on Facebook at Tet M's Photography.*

THE MAN IN GLOOM

BEATRICE AUCOIN

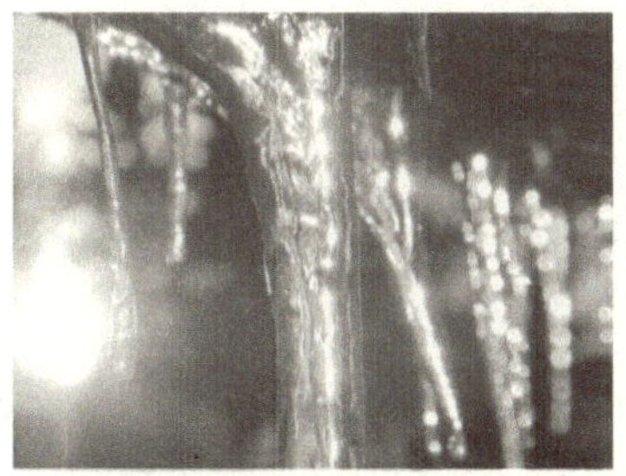

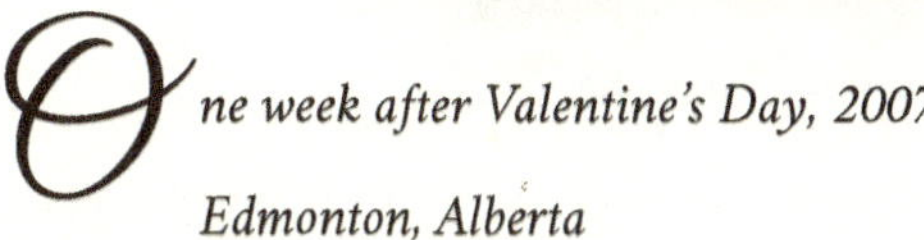

One week after Valentine's Day, 2007

Edmonton, Alberta

"Have you ever broken up with a guy and gotten back together with him?" the man asks, his voice strained with distress.

I'm enjoying a walk through the manicured and frozen Alberta Legislature grounds. The sun's just set, and the city lights glitter orange off the snow covering almost everything. My iPod plays a peppy playlist of tunes to keep my pace high as I trek through the gloom to my spouse's downtown office. We're meeting to go out together for supper.

My music's silent now, a boisterous Great Big Sea song interrupted by a whisper.

"Excuse me?"

To my right, I see a man standing a few metres away in the gloom. He can't be older than 22. His shock of black hair looks like he's rubbed his bare hands through it so many times that it's just decided to stand on end.

I take out my ear buds after his second question.

"I just broke up with my girlfriend and I'm wondering if there's a chance. I'm a guy, and I don't know much about girl stuff," he blurts out. "So I was wondering if you could tell me."

He's pleading with me, a woman he has never seen before and will never see again.

"Well," I begin, "it really depends on the circumstances of your break-up and how she feels about you."

"What if you feel low, very low?" he asks.

I don't quite understand. I answer anyway. "I wish I could give you a blanket answer, but I can't. It really depends on how she's feeling. I've been friends with exes before. I've gone back out with exes."

I flash briefly on the few times I've started dating someone after a break-up. The second-chance relationships never last long in my case.

"You're intense," I remember the last ex I went back out with saying. "It's too much. I love you, but I'm not in love with you."

I still don't know what that clichéd phrase means. If I love someone, I love them with all that I am.

That conversation is what ended that second chance; I took him at his word and decided if he was going to be part of my life, then he could be there as a friend. That didn't last long, either, because he didn't like it when I found the person I'd one day marry.

My intensity and what he'd found too much were delightful to her.

Don't go out with someone who wants to dim your brightness and tells you that you being you is too much, I think.

A partner should help you become the best version of yourself.

"But it's not the same, is it, when you go back out with someone?" the man inquires, bringing me back to the moment.

"Sometimes the feelings are deeper," I tell him. "But it's not like when you're first going out with someone because you already know that person."

I want to tell him, *Maybe she's not worth it.* Does he really want to be with someone who makes him feel so low that he's reduced to asking a random stranger on the street if there's a second chance for his ex and him?

But I'm a minor character in a short scene in his story, and he's not reached the point where he can hear that question yet.

"I wish you the best of luck," I tell him instead.

"Thanks," he says. His sneakers crunch the pathway's snow as my sight of him becomes dimmer in the gloom.

I stand there for a moment watching him before putting my ear buds back in and Great Big Sea back on. The man pauses at the next intersection, looking unsure of what to do next, as I continue in the opposite direction toward the downtown city lights to meet with my love.

~

***Beatrice Aucoin** is a queer writer originally from Cape Breton. She makes her home in downtown Calgary with her wife, Brett Bergie, and their son, Sam.* The Woman in White *is one of Beatrice's favourite novels, so she was struck by the many shades of Wilkie Collins in her encounter with the man in the gloom and his relationship questions.*

SURPRISE

PW ZELLIE

Linda and I grew up as school chums, neighbours, and best friends. We talked about all the important stuff: life, love, parents, teachers, what to do on the weekend, and of course, sex. We were both still in high school, so boys and sex were the biggest mysteries in our lives.

One year Valentine's Day fell on a Saturday so, after much contriving, we were both planning to spend the night with our boyfriends. Sadly, they cancelled on us. We were angry and confused. We decided to make the best of it though and scored ourselves some lovely Maui Wowie weed, freshly imported.

Angry and confused, we decided to make the best of it and scored ourselves some lovely Maui Wowie weed, freshly imported.

We smoked it as we walked in the cool Vancouver air, thinking that the wind would blow the smell off of us. Before long, we were cold and headed back to Linda's to bitch the night away.

We put a stack of albums on the record player, then giggled as we got into our pjs. Linda was wearing this oversized, tie-dyed t-shirt. It was so large it kept sliding off her shoulders. She looked kind of comical, but at the same time very cute. I had on an old baseball jersey that my boyfriend had given me. I would wear it to sleep in, so I could be close to him. (Ain't that sweet, but hey I was young.)

Of course we ended up talking about sex. We were lamenting the fact that the boyfriends just weren't taking us to that place we wanted to reach. We'd each been masturbating for years, but while I had experienced the "Big O," Linda hadn't.

I was telling Linda that since I had let my guy get to my pussy, he lost all interest in my chest, which I found troubling since, at least on my own, I could orgasm through my nipples.

Linda giggled, and said boob-play felt good for her, but no orgasm from that for sure. Then suddenly, she pulled up her shirt, took her right breast in both hands, and pulled it up as far as she could, bending her head down, running her tongue across her nipple.

She started laughing, and said, "Mine must be broke. No cumming from this."

Without thinking, I leaned over and took her nipple into my

mouth. I wasn't trying to seduce her. Really! It was a joke. I was just caught up in the silly moment. And did I get caught up... Linda fed me her beautiful breast with both hands. Her nipple became incredibly erect. I circled it with my tongue while my mouth covered the entire areola. I was amazed at the textures of this magnificent nipple. She pushed her chest out, responding to my attention. She groaned. I continued to suck gently, pulling her nipple into my mouth, stretching it as it hardened even more.

Linda whispered, "Yea, yea, oh God Sally, that feels so good." She slid her hand across my arm, reaching down between her legs. I moved my left hand down with hers. Her legs fell open. Now everything became instinct. I knew what worked for me. I knew what felt good. And I wanted this for Linda — I wanted sweet Linda to have the pleasure that I had enjoyed so many times on my own.

I knew that Linda's pussy was tingling. Her hand was busy, her forefinger was buried between her lips, working her clit. I slid my hand under hers. My middle finger eased down between her lips. Oh, how juicy she was. She was more than willing to allow me to take over. I felt her hips rise up to meet my fingers, as she maneuvered her pussy to give me full access to her tender nerve endings.

My mouth left her nipple and circled her entire breast, kissing every inch of its surface, spiraling out from the centre. She was so soft and smooth.

I wanted more.

I started to work my way down. Linda was gently pushing my head down her body. She knew where I was going. The rhythm of her hips quickened. I moved slowly, enjoying the taste and feel of her skin. I knew I needed to let the pleasure build. But Linda was losing control. She was far from subtle in nudging my head toward her velvety pussy. She wanted my lips on her tender lips. But I had the power, and I was going to use it — use it to tease and torture before bringing my wonderful friend to the ultimate pleasure.

Without warning, Linda slid down on the bed, legs dangling over the side. I quickly rotated myself, then eased to the floor so that I was between her legs. I knelt before her, paying homage to her sexuality, to her womanhood.

I spread Linda's legs wide, gazing at her. My tongue snaked out, traveling down her pubic bone, to the beginning of her slit. I gently worked my wet tongue down, along the folds of her labia, pushing into her vagina from above, lapping at her softness. She moaned. She was oblivious to everything but the touch of my tongue as I probed and explored. The entire focus of her being was on the pleasure radiating from her pussy. Wetness flowed from her and I let my tongue dive in, lapping it up.

Linda's taste was intoxicating. She was marvelous. I so reveled in her, loving the scent, the sensation, the glory of doing this to her, for her. It became clear to me that this beautiful pussy belonged in my mouth. As my tongue danced with her, I knew that she was meant to come alive in my mouth.

She was made for my lust.

I continued to lick her, harder now, working my head back and forth, fucking her with my mouth. I fully extended my tongue, flattened it, tilted my head upward, dragging my tongue over as much of her pussy as possible. Then I was in a frenzy, rubbing her with my nose, my forehead, my cheek-bones, my entire face... I forged up that trail of joy till I found her little bud, out of its hood, standing erect and tall. As the tip of my tongue touched it, Linda jerked involuntarily. I pulled on her clit gently with my teeth, then my lips, sucking it in, nursing it.

I had practiced on her nipple. Now my tongue was ready to dance with the queen. And dance we did.

She was the perfect partner. I thought this must be what the tango is really about, this pulse of pressure and of release. Linda's clit followed my lead to perfection. As I twisted my tongue around my little partner, Linda rhythmically swung her hips.

My tongue continued to dance with her clit, while I used my left hand to tug on her right nipple and my right hand to open her up to me. I inserted two fingers, palm side up, into her vagina. I hooked my fingers inside her, rubbing her clit from underneath. I moved them as if I was motioning her to come to me.

Come, my sweet Linda, cum to me, cum.

Linda's breathing was fast and hard. She was beyond that point of no return. She wanted it to happen NOW! I could feel that. I knew what she wanted. I knew exactly what she was experiencing.

Her muscles were beginning to contract.

Her hips were bucking wildly.

Her legs closed tight around my head, pulling me further into her. My fingers felt her vagina begin to contract, waves of contractions. I could feel her thighs squeezing my head. The waves came faster and stronger.... hips held high off the bed. Her moans became screams. Linda's entire body shook, quivered, trembled. Her muscles locked tight. I continued to lick her throbbing erect clit in frantic fast flicks, my mouth, my face covered in her rich liquid. I found it hard to breathe with her legs holding me captive, right where I wanted to be. She was lost in pleasure, and I so wanted to keep her there, in that place of overwhelming sensation and joy.

She gasped my name, "Sally, Sally, Sally. No, no more..." Her clit had become so sensitive that it was painful to the touch.

With one last groan, Linda threw her hips down, hard! She flung her legs apart, and then slammed them shut, again and again. Her body went limp.

I stopped, looked up. Crawled towards her.

In my memory I am there again, on my hands and knees over her beautiful body. She is smiling at me, the most beautiful smile I have ever seen. She reaches for me. She pulls my head to hers and kisses me. Kisses me like no one has kissed me before.

~

Cleverly disguised as a middle-aged nondescript librarian type, ***PW Zellie*** *glides through life, unremarked upon but grinning slyly, enjoying all life's yummy secrets.*

LAST

MEL VEE

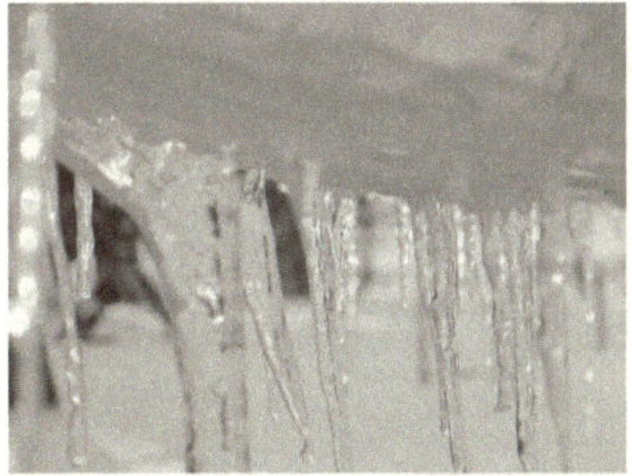

The radio blares the bluesy sweet words in the background—

This is the last car that you'll ever own, this is the last car that you'll ever own

I know you're not a car, obviously

But I wonder if you'll be my last

Swipe

Who am I kidding?

I never braved Tinder

My paralyzing fear of being murdered by strangers

Seriously cramps my ability to date people I meet online

So scratch that but maybe you'll be my last

Sigh

I'll sigh at the last pun you make

Because I'll have suffered a lifetime of your

Pun-ishments

Ok that probably wasn't very funny

But I know you won't let me laugh alone

See if I get my wish you'll be my last

Cheerleader

I think your beard would look sick with pom poms

I can't really imagine you in spandex

But even if you won't wear the outfit I still hope you're my last

Reassurance

I'm being a downer

A really, really big downer by talking about this last stuff

You'll listen patiently even when I'm a pessimist

But while we're on the subject

Imagine, for a moment, we're looking back on our lives and you were my last

Ear

To hear me complain about shit

This hospital bed sucks

I haven't watched TV since 2003 (what decade are we in again?)

I stopped being able to chew my own food 20 years ago

and I'm tired of being spoon fed hospital slop

But I'll stop

Complaining if you promise to be the last to listen to me complain like this

And we'll smile our toothless grins at each other until we have our last

Argument

Over something really stupid—

like why didn't you turn off the damn light

The light I've asked you to turn off a hundred thousand million times

Come on honey, it's one damn light! Honestly! But while we're still on the subject, our last

Fight

Will be over that time in our twenties

When I told you it's not my job to comfort your discomfort over my discomfort about your discomfort around race

And you claimed to laugh it off

But I actually thought you were pissed

We'll be grouchy for a bit, muttering under our breath to ourselves

Until our last

Laugh

Because we know we're being damned old grumpy fools

Laughing deep into our bellies

Coming up for air as we laugh-cry at our own foolishness

Meeting each other's eyes until our last

Touch

Through rickety old arthritic hands

We're both wracked with pain but we thank God

We still remember what holding hands in our twenties was like

Even if you're not my last

I'll remember how I wanted you to be

And perhaps that's the last time I'll ask for that

But I'm being a downer again

So here's to being my last, love

~

***Mel Eve** mesmerizes, captivates and incites with her spoken word. She is a passionate advocate for the power of narrative to heal and liberate. Mel Vee knows we are the gift we have been hiding from ourselves and seeks to inspire redemption, thoughtfulness, contemplation and joy through her work. She was a member of Calgary's 2017 slam team, semi-finalists at the Canadian Festival of Spoken Word, co-founding member of the Uproot YYC collective and is currently working on an anti-racist podcast through Community Wise.*

ABOUT THE PHOTOGRAPHER

LESLIE PRINGLE

The photographs illustrating *Screw Chocolate 2,* including the cover image, are all the work of Leslie Pringle. To view them in a more aesthetically appropriate size and to appreciate their glorious colour palette, visit the multimedia edition of *Screw Chocolate (1&2)* at *mjanecolette.com/ScrewChocolate* or visit Leslie's personal website *wrrldgrrl.com.*

~

***LESLIE PRINGLE** was born telling stories and hasn't stopped in over five decades. Sometimes, she uses words, sometimes photos. To enjoy more of both please go to wrrldgrrl.com.*

If she doesn't get back to you, she is probably wandering around the world, delivering school supplies and having an adventure or two.

ABOUT YYC QUEER WRITERS

S*crew Chocolate 2* is the third collaborative project by YYC Queer Writers, formed in 2013 by writer and activist Dallas Barnes. We get together intermittently to… write. Also, laud our lovers. Commiserate about our exes. Share what we wrote. Explain what we want to write. Try to justify why we aren't writing it. Go home and write it. Come back. Share it… repeat.

We believe telling and sharing stories is how we change the world.

~

In YYC and want to write with us? Find us on Facebook at Calgary Queer Writing Group or send us a note through *mjanecolette.com/yycqueerwriters*.

MORE PROJECTS

BY YYC QUEER WRITERS

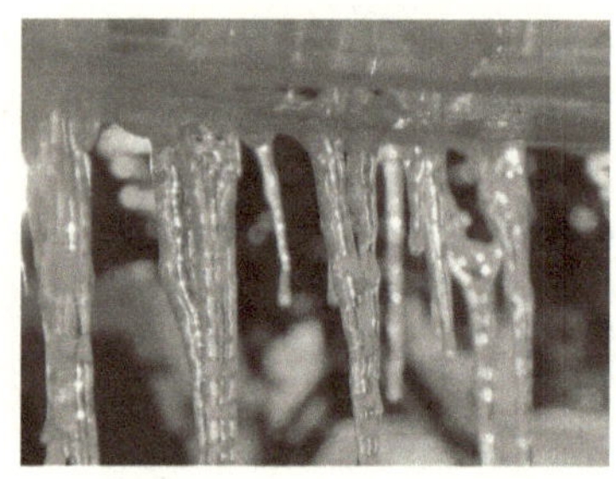

- *Screw Chocolate: 14 QUEER valentines to get you through February 14*, February 2017
- *Queer Christmas in Cowtown,* December 2017
- *Screw Chocolate 2,* February 2018
- *Queer Christmas In Cowtown*: theme to be determined, coming December 2018 (submissions open)
- *On A Queer Summer's Night in Calgary*, coming July 2019 (submissions open)

Interested in contributing? Go to *mjanecolette.com/yycqueerwriters* for details.